# THE LIFE OF

# ROBERT OWEN

PHILANTHROPIST AND SOCIAL REFORMER

## AN APPRECIATION

BY

## R. E. DAVIES

LONDON
ROBERT SUTTON, 43 THE EXCHANGE
SOUTHWARK

—

1907

'Born humbly, like the greatest of earth's sons,
His genius found the means to curve his way.
His goal, no vulgar one, no cult of gold,
Riches came to him unsolicited,
As 'twere impelled by hand invisible.
These valued he at their intrinsic worth,
At most, a power of lessening human ills.
Philanthropist he was, and without cant,
Or fads, or humbug, that blinds not but fools,
He practised in his life the Christ idea
Of altruism and self-sacrifice
That some but prate of.'

# Robert Owen

ROBERT OWEN, the father of English Socialism, was the son of Robert Owen, saddler, ironmonger, and postmaster at Newtown, Montgomeryshire, and Anne his wife. He was born on the 14th May, 1771, and was the youngest but one of seven children. When very young he attended school kept in Newtown Hall, and at the age of seven had received all the instruction required in that primitive time, and so became usher. His ushership served to pay for his schooling. Owen, in his 'Autobiography,' gives some interesting reminiscences of his schooldays. He says : 'I recollect being very anxious to be first in school and first home, and the boys had always a race from the school to the town, and being a fast runner I was usually at home first, and almost always the first at school in the morning. On one occasion my haste nearly cost me my life. I used to have for breakfast a basin of flummery,* and I requested that this breakfast might be always ready when I returned from school so that I might eat it speedily in order to be the first back again to school.† One morning, when about five years old, I ran home as usual from school, found my basin of flummery ready, and, as I supposed, sufficiently cold for eating, for no heat appeared to arise from it. It had skimmed over as when quite cold; but on my hastily taking a spoonful of it I found it was quite scalding hot, the body of it retaining all its heat. The consequence was instant fainting from the stomach being scalded. In that state I remained so long that my parents thought life was extinct. However, after a considerable period I revived, but from that day my stomach became incapable of digesting food, except the most simple and

---

* A kind of porridge.

† This shows incidentally that in those days children went to school before breakfast.

in small quantities at a time. This made me attend to the effects of different qualities of food on my changed constitution, and gave me the habit of close observation and of continued reflection, and I have always thought that this accident had a great influence in forming my character.'

When he had attained the age of ten, Owen left Newtown for London ' with my habits of reflection and extreme temperance,' as he says, 'not liking the habits and manners of a small country town.' The journey to London was rather a formidable undertaking in those days for a lad's start in life ; but with the proud consciousness of forty shillings of his own in his pocket, young Owen endured with equanimity the infliction of an outside ride on a night-running coach.

In London he remained a few weeks with his eldest brother, William, a saddler, in Holborn, after which he obtained a situation with Mr. James McGuffog, in a respectable drapery establishment at 36 St. Mary Street, Stamford, Lincolnshire, where he spent three years. His wages, according to his agreement, were to be nothing for the first year, £8 for the second, and £10 for the third. Owen states that among his employer's customers were some of the highest nobility in the kingdom, 'and often six or seven carriages belonging to them were at the same time in attendance upon the premises. His shop was, in fact, a kind of town rendezvous for the nobility and principal gentry of the neighbourhood, when they visited the town.'

Owen had a happy time whilst with Mr. McGuffog. He earned the esteem and enjoyed the confidence of his employer. There was a well-filled library in the house, and the business left plenty of spare time in which to indulge in study.

After leaving Stamford, Owen obtained a situation in a haberdasher's shop (Messrs. Flint and Palmer's) on Old London Bridge, where he felt himself 'rich and independent' on £25 a year, with board and lodging. This was a hard place.

With his fellow-assistants he had to be in
the shop, with breakfasts already stowed
away, by 8 o'clock in the morning, and
they were kept under the harrow until 11
at night, with the prospect of straightening
up stock, perhaps for two or three hours
more after that. Small wonder that he
says he was sometimes ' scarcely able, with
the help of the banisters, to go upstairs to
bed.'

All the assistants had every morning
to pass under the hand of the barber before
entering the shop. ' Boy as I was,' writes
Owen, 'I had to wait my turn for the
hairdresser to powder, pomatum, and curl
my hair, for I had two large curls on
each side, and a stiff pigtail, and until this
was very nicely done no one could think
of appearing before a customer.' They
wore stocks too, and skin-tight breeches,
those trim and trussed assistants, and how
they endured fifteen to eighteen hours of
such shackled activity passeth comprehen-
sion. He did not remain long in this
situation, but bettered himself by taking a

similar position at Mr. Satterfield's, in St. Ann's Square, Manchester, where he received £40 a year.

Whilst in the latter place Owen became acquainted with a mechanic named Jones, who persuaded him to become a partner with him in the manufacture of mules for spinning cotton, a recent invention of Crompton's. The capital was £100, and the materials were obtained on credit. England at this time was, industrially, very primitive. The manufacture of cotton was carried on with the aid of the one-thread spinning wheel, along with the old hand-loom, with its fly shuttle, invented by John Kaye, of Bury. Steam had not begun its mighty work, and motive power was obtained from wind and water.

The partnership between Owen and Jones soon proved unsatisfactory, and was dissolved, and for some time Owen carried on himself in Ancoats Lane, Manchester, the business of spinning cotton yarn or thread. With a small plant of three mules, a reel, and a making-up machine, and the help of three men, he bought cotton rovings to be spun into yarn, giving 12s. a pound for the rough, and getting 22s. a pound for the finished product. In this way he made a profit of about six pounds a week.

When but nineteen years of age, Owen obtained a situation as manager to a large cotton mill, where over five hundred men were employed, belonging to one Mr. Drinkwater, who took to all his machinery at cost price, and agreed to pay him a salary of £300 a year. At the time Owen entered upon this responsible office he was almost entirely ignorant of the business, but he soon mastered it, and brought the mill into superior order. His employer was so pleased with his conduct that in three years he had increased his salary to £500.

The mill Owen was now managing was the first that had ever been erected for fine cotton spinning by machinery. He raised the standard of quality and fineness of the yarn produced until it reached a price

50 per cent. in excess of the list, and in place of 120 hanks to the pound, which was the highest made before him, he succeeded in reaching 250 and later 300 hanks to the pound. It is also worthy of note that Owen was the first to manufacture thread from Sea Island North American cotton—an article which afterwards came so much in demand. His name soon became known as the first fine cotton spinner in the world.

Mr. Drinkwater had promised Owen at the expiration of the third year of his engagement a partnership on equal sharing terms with himself and his two sons, then nearing manhood. But this arrangement was never carried into effect, for a young spinner, who was about to marry Mr. Drinkwater's daughter, objected to a share in the business being held by anyone but a member of the family. Owen was thereupon asked to name his own salary on condition of relinquishing the agreement, but he declined to stop on sufferance upon any terms. The account he gives of the circumstances under which he left Mr. Drinkwater's service is very characteristic. One day Mr. Drinkwater sent for him and told him : 'I have sent for you that I may explain unexpected changes which have taken place lately in my family. The celebrated Mr. Oldknow is to become my son-in-law. You know he is the first British muslin manufacturer, and he is becoming a great cotton spinner. He has expressed a strong wish that the entire business of both families should be retained in the family, but you are entitled by our agreement to become a partner in my mills next year, and this agreement obstructs his extensive views and arrangements. He wishes me to ascertain from you on what conditions you would retain the management of my mills, and give up the agreement for a partnership in our business. If you will give up your claim to the partnership you may name your own salary. You have now £500 a year, and whatever sum you name you shall have.'

Owen, in reply, said : ' I have brought the agreement with me, and here it is, and I now put it into the fire, because I never will connect myself with any parties who are not desirous to be united with me ; but under these circumstances I cannot remain your manager with any salary you can give ; ' and the agreement was consumed before him.   It was a bold, and possibly injudicious, step to take ; but Owen must, at this time, have had a fair idea of his own value.   With the improvement he had effected in the counts of yarn he had been allowed to place his own name on the bundles, and these had come to bear the highest value in the market.   He was recognised, not merely as an efficient, but an extremely able man, and when it became known that he was at liberty he was offered a third share in the business of another large manufacturer, Samuel Marsland, but would not join under equal shares in the profits.   An agreement in those terms was almost come to with another firm ; but before it was ratified Owen joined Messrs.

Borrowdale and Atkinson, under the firm of 'The Chorlton Twist Company,' sharing the management with a brother of one of partners.

It became part of his duty to sell a portion of the yarn produced, and during a business visit to Glasgow he became acquainted with Mr. David Dale, a banker and proprietor of extensive cotton mills* and village at New Lanark, and formerly a partner of Richard Arkwright, the inventor. Finding Mr. Dale anxious to dispose of his business, then reported to be the largest of the kind in the kingdom, Owen persuaded his partners to dispose of the mills at Manchester and purchase the concern at a cost of £60,000, payable in twenty equal annual instalments, and was installed there as resident manager at a salary of £1,000 per annum and one-ninth of the profits besides. The title of the new firm was 'The New Lanark Twist Company.'

---

* These mills were founded in 1784 near the Falls of the Clyde, in order to utilise the water power.

This occurred in the summer of 1797, when Owen was twenty-six years of age.

Owen's connection with Manchester was not of business alone, for he succeeded in entering into the intellectual and educational life of the city in a manner little short of marvellous. He became very early on a member of the Manchester Literary and Philosophical Society, thus obtaining an introduction to the best society. It was at one of the meetings of this Society that he made his first effort in oratory. Here it was that, scarce out of his teens, he first became acquainted with John Dalton, Manchester's famous chemist, an acquaintance that ripened into firm friendship, for Owen made a great impression on Dalton's as on other cultured minds. It was also at one of the Society's meetings that Owen laid it down that all the universe was one great laboratory ; that all things were chemical compounds, and that man was only a complicated chemical compound ; that he acquired .thenceforth the *soubriquet* of ' the philosopher who intended to make men by chemistry.'

When the poet Coleridge was on a visit to Manchester he attended a gathering of the Literary and Philosophical Society, and Owen had the courage to enter into public debate with him. This encounter gained for him the title of the 'reasoning machine.' Long afterwards, when again they met, Coleridge reminded Owen of this encounter, and remarked that though he (Coleridge) had on his side fluency and oratorical accomplishments, Owen had certainly on his side what was more desirable—reason.

On the 30th September, 1799, Owen married Mr. Dale's daughter. His account of the wedding, which was conducted according to the Scottish custom, is of an amusing character. He describes how they were assembled in the house of the bride's father. Mr. Balfour, an old friend of the family, was asked to perform the ceremony, upon which he requested the bride and bridegroom to stand up, and asked them if they were willing to take each other for husband and wife. They nodded assent, and without a word more the minister said, 'Then you are married and you may sit down.'

Soon after his marriage Owen commenced expounding his views upon the question of education, which he desired taken up by the nation. He was impressed with the conviction that it was criminal in a very high degree to appropriàte the wealth then rapidly accumulating and the power it brought with it to the creation of large private fortunes to the growth or the exaltation of one class. It was in this belief that he began his labours. The keynote of his action can best be given by an extract from his own writings. He says : 'Observe the different appearances, bodily and mentally, which the inhabitants of the various regions of the earth present. Are they inherited in our nature, or do they arise from the respective soils on which we are born ? Evidently from neither. They are wholly and solely the effect of education. Man becomes a ferocious savage, a cannibal, or a highly civilized and benevolent being, according to the circumstances in which he may be placed from his birth. If any given number of children were exchanged at birth between the society of friends and the loose fraternity of St. Giles, in London, the children of the former would grow up like the members of the latter, prepared for any degree of crime; while those of the latter would become the same temperate, good, moral characters as the former.' Owen saw, as no man before him had seen, that environment is the maker of men. John Bradford, upon seeing a prisoner led to execution, exclaimed, There goes John Bradford —but for the grace of God.' He might have said with equal truthfulness, ' There goes John Bradford—but for better parentage, the advantages of sweeter surroundings, and the benefit of thorough education.' It is now generally recognised that hereditary taint and unwholesome environment—especially the latter—are largely responsible for the crime of this country. We are all animals, however high we may be in the scale of creation, and the more judiciously we are bred, the better (in the aggregate) we shall prove. Such attributes as courage, magnanimity, truthfulness, and perseverance can be, and are, passed on to posterity on the one hand ; and such curses as drunkenness, diseases, and inclination to criminality may be bequeathed on the other ; but in all these cases the environment, influence, and training form primary factors for the future good or evil of the individual. Aristotle asked, ' Character is destiny, but how can character be made ?' The only material way known in Owen's day was by prayer and precept. Owen said there were material means largely unused which were conducive, or might be made conducive, to human improvement, and the spirit of Browning's prayer, ' Make no more giants, God, but elevate the race at once,' was his aim. Taking these ideas as fundamental principles, he at once arrayed against him the strong Calvinistic community, in the midst of which he sought to work a social revolution.

About the year 1800 Owen expended large sums of money in erecting a new village for the workpeople, and schools for the five hundred children at New Lanark (principally paupers, procured from the surrounding parishes), 'taking as much care of the living machinery as of the dead,' as he expressed it. The school teachers were selected not so much for their high intellectual acquirements as for their even temper, patience, and strong love for children. They were instructed never to permit their pupils to hear angry words spoken, nor to weary them by teachings unsuited to their age or capacity. The school age began at two years, and children sometimes hardly strong enough to walk were carried there. No books were used in teaching the very young. They were taught the nature and use of common things by familiar conversation. Dancing lessons were commenced at three years of

age, singing lessons at four years and upwards. Both sexes were drilled in military
exercises, being formed into divisions, led
by a drum and fife band, composed of boys
in the upper department. The classes for
the advanced pupils also received great
attention, and the system of teaching in use
was considered far in advance of anything
known or practised at the time. At first
education was free, and was given to all
children up to ten years of age, but afterwards a nominal fee (threepence per month
for each child) was charged to keep the benefit free from the taint of charity.

'The institution for the formation of
character,' as Owen termed the schools,
soon became the wonder of the world, and
visitors arrived 'not by hundreds, but by
thousands annually.' 'I have seen,' wrote
Owen, 'as many as seventy strangers at
once attending the early morning exercises
of the children in the school.'

The Duke of Kent, the father of Her
late Majesty Queen Victoria, sent his
physician, Dr. McNab, to see the schools,

who reported in terms of wonder and admiration. 'No language,' said Lord Torrington, 'can do justice to the excellence of the arrangements in that establishment. At New Lanark, Mr. Owen has frequently a meeting of from 1,000 to 1,200 persons, 800 of them from sixteen to twenty years of age, all uniting in friendly conversation, accompanied by some instrumental music.'

Besides many English notabilities who visited New Lanark, there came the Duke of Holstein and his brother ; Princes John and Maximilian of Austria ; the Grand Duke of Oldenburgh, and many foreign ambassadors, among others Baron Just, Ambassador of Saxony, whose Sovereign presented Owen with a gold medal as a mark of approval.

The Grand Duke Nicholas, afterwards Emperor of Russia, with his suite, also visited the village and schools. At that time there was a great commotion about the doctrines of Malthus. Owen relates that 'in a two hours' conversation with the

Grand Duke, before he left, he said : " As
your country is overpeopled, I will take
you and two millions of population with
you, all in similar manufacturing commu-
nities." ' This was certainly a most extra-
ordinary offer on the part of the most
arbitrary, despotic monarch in the world,
for the New Lanark community was based
upon ' liberty, equality, fraternity.' Owen,
however, declined, as he thought his hands
were full enough of work at the time.

Of the village itself, an American
traveller declared : ' There is not, I appre-
hend, to be found in any part of the world
a manufacturing village in which so much
order, good government, tranquillity, and
rational happiness prevail.'

By moral suasion and the removal of
pot-houses, drunkenness had been reduced
to a minimum ; by imposing ingenious
checks he put a stop to systematic pilfering
which had formerly been carried on almost
with impunity, and a detected thief was
punished by scorn instead of prosecution.
A curious means of maintaining discipline,

or, as Owen described it, ' the most effec-
tive check upon inferior conduct,' had been
established throughout the mills. ' This
consisted of a four-sided piece of wood,
about two inches long and one broad, each
side coloured, one side black, another blue,
the third yellow, and the fourth white,
tapered at the top, aud finished with wire
eyes to hang upon a hook, with either side
to the front. One of these was suspended
in a conspicuous place near to each of the
persons employed, and the colour to the
front told the conduct of the individual
during the preceding days to four degrees
of comparison ; bad denoted by black, or
No. 4 ; indifferent by blue, or No. 3 ; good
by yellow, or No. 2 ; excellent by white,
or No: 1. Then books of character were
provided for each department, in which
the name of each one employed in it was
inserted, which sufficed to mark by the
numbers the daily conduct for two months ;
and these books were changed six times a
year and were preserved ; by which arrangement I had the conduct of each registered to

four degrees of comparison every day of
the week, Sundays excepted, for every year
they remained in my employment. The
superintendent of each department had
the placing daily of these silent monitors,
and the master of the mill regulated those
of the superintendents in each mill. At
the commencement of this new method of
recording character the great majority were
black, many blue, and a few yellow.
Gradually the black diminished and were
succeeded by the blue, and the blue were
gradually succeeded by the yellow ; and
some, but at first very few, were white.'

What would be thought or said of the
introduction of such a plan as this in any
mercantile establishment to-day ?

But other reforms of Owen's took a
more practical turn. He opened a shop
for the supply of all kinds of necessaries
at cost price, although in later years a
profit was levied large enough to cover the
expenses of education. Such a step may
quite likely have been expedient in regard
to the circumstances of an out-of-the-way

village in those days, and was, of course, more of a charitable measure than actual co-operation, although that system, on lines more nearly approaching its present development, afterwards was made part and parcel of his propaganda.

In addition to consideration of the resources of his workpeople, Owen provided recreation and instruction for them and looked closely—more closely than workers would suffer now—into their morals and behaviour. A paternal interest was taken in finding suitable and constant employment for them. He opened a public kitchen and dining room, by which the waste of separate cooking was avoided ; and calculated that the people saved by this means no less than four to five thousand pounds a year. In the upper storey of the new building there was a library, reading, and ball rooms ; the whole was heated by hot air. But his principal care was for his schools, in which he hoped to foster character and education together, and upon the schools he lavished time, thought, and money.

Strange, however, to relate, Owen's work at New Lanark was constantly hindered and opposed, at first by the clergy in the neighbourhood, and later by many over the entire country. He was also distrusted by the operatives, who credited him only with an eye to profit mongery in his reforms.

In 1806, in consequence of differences between the United States Government and ours, the former laid an embargo on their own ports, and no cotton was allowed to be exported. Prices immediately advanced so rapidly that manufacturers stopped their machinery rather than continue to work the material at the high price it had attained, and run the risk of a sudden fall in the price should the embargo be removed. Owen closed the New Lanark mills, but retained the operatives, and continued to pay them their full wages as long as the embargo was maintained. During this period, which was of four months duration, the population received more than £7,000 for their unemployed time. This won for him the hearts of the work-people.

Some of his partners being unable to acquiesce in his operations, Owen, in 1809, paid them £84,000 for their interest in the company, and became the sole proprietor for a short time. He afterwards admitted fresh partners into the concern, but from these he soon met with much opposition.

Continual frictions culminated in another sale of the works by public auction in 1813, when Owen, in conjunction with Jeremy Bentham and half-a-dozen other gentlemen, again became the buyer at £114,110. The sale took place in Glasgow, and as soon as the bargain was settled, scouts set out to notify the inhabitants of New Lanark of Owen's coming. They, in turn, sallied forth to meet his carriage, which, having unyoked the horses, they hauled in triumph to the village—a tribute which touched him deeply, and, if possible, increased his determination to do them and the children all the good in his power.

A new company was again formed, but on the express condition that Owen was to work his will so long as the mills paid his partners five per cent.

About this time (1813) Owen published his views in the form of a collection of essays, entitled, 'A New View of Society, or Essays on the Formation of Human Character.' These essays strike the dominant note of Owen's philosophy. They argue that the 'character of man is formed *for* him and not *by* him,' or as it was afterwards amplified as the ruling motto on the title page of later publications—

'The formation of man's character is most essentially determined by the external circumstances which are made to influence him before and from his birth, and by which he is caused to acquire correct and beneficial or erroneous and injurious ideas ; and now, through the guidance of the newly-attained science of the effects of external circumstances upon man, these circumstances may easily be so ordered by society as to determine the formation of a highly superior character, including correct and beneficial ideas, in all—a character of general excellence, in wisdom and goodness; but endlessly varied individually according to the diversities of innate physical and mental constitution.'

The essays went through many editions, and attracted general attention. They brought Owen into intimate acquaintance with the Archbishop of Canterbury, Lord Liverpool, Wilberforce, Macintosh, Malthus, and other leading men of the time, and also secured him a friendly interview with the Premier. The King of Prussia wrote him an autograph letter of thanks for the pleasure of reading them, and the United States Minister asked for enough to enable one to be sent to the Governor of every State in the Union, and Lord Sidmouth ordered one to be sent to each of the Bishops.

In 1814 Owen exerted himself to rouse public opinion to consider the lamentable condition of young children employed

in factories, in which he encountered strong
opposition from interested millowners. At
that time, according to Owen, 'every man
did that which was right in his own eyes,
and vice and immorality prevailed to a
monstrous extent.' The labour of young
people being a necessity in certain branches
of factory industry, and owing to a strong
indisposition existing on the part of the
parents in some localities to allow their
children to enter the mill gates, the plan
resorted to was to obtain as apprentices from
the various workhouses of the kingdom
as large a number of the pauper children
as were required, and bind them under
indenture. As Lloyd Jones says, 'they
were bargained for, and sent to their desti-
nation in droves ; the workhouse authorities, glad enough to get rid of them,
prudently stipulating that those who con-
tracted for them should take a due propor-
tion of the ailing and idiotic.' Housed in
sheds, their food was not only of the
poorest kind, but frequently insufficient,
while the beds in which they slept were

said never to get cold, for as those on
the day-shift rose to begin their labours,
those coming off the night-shift took their
places under what did duty for blankets.
Unable to look after themselves, and with
no one to care whether they lived or died,
these poor creatures were entirely at the
mercy of those put in charge of them.
Their treatment has been regarded as
heart-rending in the extreme, for in addition to being half-starved and neglected,
they were often flogged in order that they
might keep awake when nature's force had
spent itself. Little wonder, therefore, that
the ceaseless drudgery hurried them in
crowds to their graves. A Bill was prepared by Owen in 1816, which the first
Sir Robert Peel introduced into Parliament, for the purpose of regulating the
employment of children in factories, and
providing for their education. This Bill
proposed to limit the time of working to
ten hours a day, and the age of admission
to twelve; to provide for the instruction
of children before their admission, and

for the keeping of factories clean and well ventilated. After some delays, it was referred to a Select Committee, but encountered such strong opposition from the manufacturers that although in 1818 it finally became law it was in such a mutilated form as to be of very little good.

In an address by Owen to the cotton manufacturers of the United Kingdom he says : ' Many of you have long experienced in your manfacturing operations the advantage of substantial, well-contrived, and well-executed machinery. Experience has also shown you the difference of results between mechanism which is neat and clean, well arranged and always in a high state of repair, and that which is allowed to be dirty, in disorder, without the means of preventing unnecessary friction, and which, therefore, becomes and works much out of repair. In the first case the whole economy and management are good. Every operation proceeds with ease, order, and success ; in the last the reverse must follow, and a scene be presented of counter

action, confusion, and dissatisfaction among
all the agents and instruments interested or
occupied in the general process which cannot fail to create great loss. If this due
care as to the state of your inanimate
machines can produce such beneficial results, what may not be expected if you
devote equal attention to your vital
machinery, which are far more wonderfully
constructed. When you shall acquire a
right knowledge of these, of their curious
mechanism, of their self-adjusting powers,
when the proper mainspring shall be
applied to their varied movements, you
will become conscious of their actual value
and you will readily be induced to turn your
thoughts more frequently from your inanimate to your living machines.'

Owen gave evidence before the Committee of the House of Commons, which
sat to report upon the Relief of the Manufacturing and Labouring Poor, and his
suggestions which appeared in their report
of 1817, revealed his socialism. He anti-
cipated at the beginning of the new industry

all the evils evolved in its subsequent
development, and saw especially that the
machinery which was meant to bless man
would first curse him. In his 'Observations on the Effects of the Manufacturing
System ' (1817) he says : ' Since the dis-
covery of the enormous, the incalculable
power to supersede manual labour, to
enable the human race to create wealth by
the aid of the sciences, it has been a gross
mistake of the political economists to make
humanity into slaves to science, instead
of making, as Nature intends, science
to be the slave and the servant of
humanity. And this sacrificing of human
beings, with such exquisite physical,
intellectual, moral, spiritual, and practical
organs, faculties and powers, so wondrously
contained in each individual, to pins,
needles, thread, tape, etc., and to all such
inanimate materials, exhibits at once the
most gross ignorance of the nature and
true value of humanity, and of the principles and practices required to form a
prosperous, rational, and happy state of

society, or the true existence of man upon earth.' He even goes so far as to ask where the increased wealth went which his two thousand workpeople produced— wealth which it would have taken six hundred thousand men to have produced a century before. He clearly saw that his people benefited but little. Owen revolted then against the subordination of man to machinery, which he saw going on around him.

Nor was he satisfied with Malthus's solution. He denied that over-population was any danger, he saw that the efficiency of the means of production would increase in greater ratio, and declared that it was not by artificially limiting population that men could escape from their woes, but 'by instituting rational arrangements and by securing a fair distribution of wealth.'

In 1816 Owen gave to the King of Prussia an outline of a national system of education, which was put into practice the following year. The Dutch system of pauper management was also founded on his recommendations. It was chiefly through Owen that Lord Brougham, James Mill, and Sir C. Grey opened in 1819, in Brewer's Green, Westminster, the first public infant school in England, on similar lines to those of New Lanark. This venture met with less success than the former one, but the work once begun was never allowed to drop. Owen also gave £1,000 to Joseph Lancaster, the Quaker, in order to help him in the work of forming British schools ; £500 to Bell, who was the originator of Church or National Schools, and offered to make the £500 a £1,000 if Bell would agree to admit Nonconformist children into the Church Schools.*

---

* In 1871, at the centenary celebration of Owen's birth, Professor Huxley said : 'It is my duty to take part in the attempt which the country is now making (the great school board contest) to carry into effect some of Robert Owen's most cherished schemes. No one can look into the problem of popular education but he must be led to Owen's conclusion that the infant school is, so to speak, the key of the position. Robert Owen discerned this great fact, and with courage and patience worked out his theory into practice, and that is his great claim, if he had no other, to the enduring gratitude of mankind.'

In the summer of 1817 he held a series of crowded public meetings at the London Tavern for the purpose of expounding his schemes for the amelioration of the human race, and for governing the affairs of men. Having, at one of these meetings, denounced all the religions of the world as injurious to mankind, most of the influential classes entirely deserted him, and he at once lost much of his popularity.

About this time Saint Simon propounded his Socialist views in France in his treatise, 'L'Industrie.' Saint Simon's Socialism was somewhat sentimental and theoretic, a result of the French Revolution, and a deduction from the abstract principles of 'liberty, equality, and fraternity.' Robert Owen's, on the other hand, was practical, and arose from no abstract principles, but directly from the heart and heat of the New Industry itself. It was truer Socialism, inasmuch as it was of industrial and not of political origin, the direct product of the Industrial Revolution.

Owen stood as a candidate for Parliament in 1819 for the Lanark Burghs, but he never took much interest in any political reforms.

In 1821 he started a journal, *The Economist*, in which to advocate his cause. The spirit in which he entered on his enterprise may be gathered from these glowing words in the first number : 'I have had the boldness to take upon my shoulders the burden of examining the whole affairs and circumstances of mankind. . . . . . I summon to my aid all the friends of humanity. If my feeble voice be at first scarcely heard amid the noisy contentions of the world, yet, if it be joined by the full chorus of the sons of truth, swelling into clarion shouts of countless multitudes, and caught with joyous acclaim from nation to nation, the harmonising strains shall resound throughout the globe.' On the title page of his paper it was declared to be 'a periodical paper, explanatory of a new system of society and a plan of association for improving the condition of the working classes during their continuance at their present employment.'

Owen was now persuaded that he had found a cure for all our woes, and visited France, Switzerland, Germany, and many other parts of the Continent, where he was well received by Cuvier, Louis Phillippe, Oberlin, Humboldt, and other eminent men. On his return to England he found that by his attacks on religion he was looked upon by many as an avowed infidel. He became at once an apostle and a martyr.

All this time New Lanark had continued to prosper, both financially and otherwise, and the establishment grew into one of vast proportions, until the population reached 2,500 persons, all acting entirely under Owen's directions. In a letter to the *Times* in 1834, he said, addressing his friend, Lord Brougham : 'I believe it is known to your lordship that from every point of view no experiment was ever so successful as the one I conducted at New Lanark, although it was commenced and

continued in opposition to all the oldest
and strongest prejudices of mankind. For
twenty-five years we did without the necessity for magistrates or lawyers ; without a
single legal punishment ; without any
known poor-rate ; without intemperance
and religious animosities. We reduced
the hours of labour, well educated the
children from infancy, greatly improved
the conditions of adults, paid interest on
capital, and cleared upwards of £300,000
of profit.' Disagreements, however, arose
between Owen and his partners. One of
them, William Allen, a very conscientious
and well-intended man, very rich, a great
philanthropist, and with great influence,
annoyed Owen very much, setting his own
Quaker views and beliefs up as a standard
by which to judge him. He condemned
the policy of the whole educational system,
particularly the teaching of dancing, singing, and drilling, and the use of the High-
land costume. These in his eyes were all
exceedingly improper. They poisoned the
mind with lightness and vanity, with a

taste for military display, and instilled into the mind of the young a desire for the glory of the battlefield ; the naked legs of the children shocked his sense of propriety and foreshadowed to his narrow mind immorality in after life. He also considered the placing in the hands of the people such works as Shakespeare's writings and novels and romances of any kind as a dangerous experiment, and having a strong tendency to immorality ; and so set himself against the matter and carried his point, Owen with great regret withdrawing from the company. It was not, however, until 1829 that he broke off all his connection with New Lanark.

After the mills changed hands there were sore years for the workpeople ; wages were cut down, despite the fact that the new company made handsome profits out of the business. Starvation was common, and as almost everything was bought on the truck system, after accounts were squared at the end of each month between the workers and the employers, five pounds would almost be enough to pay the difference.

In 1825 Owen went to America, where he purchased 30,000 acres of fertile land in Illinois and Indiana, on the river Wabash, and founded at the cost of £40,000 to himself, New Harmony, a model Commune, while his disciple, Abraham Combe, set up another for him at Orbiston, near Glasgow. Both experiments were utter failures, and caused the financial ruin of Owen, who, with heroic self-sacrifice, sank a whole fortune in them. He also founded settlements on communistic and beautifully-adjusted regulations at Balahine, county Clare, Ireland, in 1831, and at Harmony Hall, Tytherley, Hampshire, in 1839 ; which all ended in failure as soon as human nature began to get free play.

Nothing daunted, he resolved to devote himself to the instruction of the working classes in London, to prepare them for the mighty changes he still hoped to effect. His followers—the Owenites—recruited from the tailor's shop, the smithy, the cobbler's bench, the manufactory, the ploughtail, and from every place where the sons of toil had learned to read and think—did start labour leagues, but the fruit they produced was political, they produced the Chartist agitation.

The following is a copy of an advertisement of Owen's lectures, taken from a London newspaper in 1829 :—

' A Cure for Want, or the Fear of Want. Attend Mr. Owen's Lectures, delivered every Sunday morning, at 11 o'clock, at No. 2 Leicester Place, Leicester Square, and judge for yourselves of the principles on which Mr. Owen proposes to found an entire New State of Society, in which Truth will be substituted for Religion, beneficial realities for injurious mysteries and ceremonies ; knowledge for ignorance ; riches for poverty ; universal charity, kind feelings, and union, for discord, evil passions, unkind feelings, and uncharitableness. You who wish to avoid Want, or fear of Want, and to prevent the longer existence of the cut-throat work that now pervades all ranks of Society, if you cannot attend the Lectures, read and study them, and then judge for yourselves of the practicability of Owen's principles of Society ; you will then be convinced that Want, or the fear of it, can be easily banished from the earth.

'Owen's Lectures are published weekly by Strange, Paternoster Row ; and H. Hetherton, No. 13 King's Gate Street, Holborn, in numbers, price 3d. each ; and to be had of every Bookseller.'

In 1832 he established a penny weekly paper called the *Crisis*, also an ' Equitable Labour Exchange,' where notes for work done were to supersede money. The latter came to a disastrous close, about the end of 1833 ; there being a confessed deficiency of about £2,500, the whole of which Owen paid himself.

In 1835 the Owenites first gave the name ' Socialism ' to the new movement at meetings of 'the association of all classes and of all nations.' Owen's Socialism however came too soon, not for the need of the workmen, but for his intelligence. In 1839 the *Westminster Review* stated that Robert Owen's Secularism was the actual creed of a great portion of the working classes of this country.

In 1840 Owen was presented at Court by Lord Melbourne—a proceeding which drew forth from the redoubtable Bishop of Exeter (Dr. Philpotts) one of his bitterest declamations.

From this date, for some years, little was heard of Owen. His ambitious scheme for 'the reconstruction of society' had proved a failure, and gradually his existence was almost forgotten except by the small circle of Socialists or Co-operators, who still looked to him as their prophet and from time to time assembled to do him honour.

At the Great Exhibition in Hyde Park he read an address to 'The Delegates of the Human Race met at the World's Fair

in the Crystal Palace in the British Metro-
polis in 1851.'

About the year 1853 Owen was con-
verted to Spiritualism, and over this portion of his life any disciple of his, as well
as those who admire his many good qualities and applaud his self-denying efforts on
behalf of others, would gladly draw a veil.
He became a firm believer in apparitions
and spirit-rapping, and asserted that he
received frequent visits from the spirits of
the Duke of Kent and others of his old
friends—that he had been specially selected
by them to reveal their secrets to a wretched
world, to convince it of error, and to save
it from that chaos into which it had fallen.
His finally renouncing secularism for what
one calls 'the comfortless vagaries' of
spiritualism, was probably due to the influence of his eldest son, Robert Dale Owen,*
the American Senator and Spiritualist.

---

* R. D. Owen, philosopher and novelist, was born 1804.
He went with his father to America in 1823, settled in Indiana,
and represented it in Congress, and was *chargé d'affairs* at Naples
from 1853 to 1858. Among his works are 'Hints on Archi-
tecture,' Beyond the Breakers,' and 'Threading My Way.'

The last appearance in public of Robert
Owen was at a meeting of the Social
Science Congress in Liverpool in October,
1858, when he was introduced by his old
friend Lord Brougham, and read a paper,
entitled, 'The Human Race Governed
Without Punishment.' He almost immediately afterwards broke down, and came
to Newtown on the 8th November following, accompanied by his secretary (Mr.
Rigby), and sought accommodation in the
house in which he was born. This not
being obtainable, he put up at the Bear's
Head Hotel,

> 'And as an hare, whom hounds and horns pursue.
> Pants for the place from whence at first it flew,'

so he fully resolved to spend his few
remaining days in his native town and to
die there.

This happened on the 17th of the
same month. By his own desire, his body
was placed in the room wherein he was
born, and hundreds of persons went to see
it. The funeral, which was a very large
one, was attended by twelve chief mourners

and twelve of the oldest men in the town, two of whom had been his schoolmates. Then came twelve schoolboys, who had been supplied with caps and coats, after whom came twelve tradesmen, followed by the general public. Thus, after a long life of nearly 88 years, and after roaming nearly all over the world, Owen was permitted to spend the last few days of his eventful life, and to die within a few yards of where he was born, and in the dingy old churchyard of his native town, beside the ashes of his forefathers, he lies buried.

In 1868, a proposal was made for the erection of a monument to the memory of Robert Owen at Newtown, and the Local Board was applied to by some of his admirers for permission for the erection of a monument in some prominent position in the town. They gave a decided negative to the proposal, and from correspondence which appeared in the public prints at the time, such refusal was stated to be grounded on the irreligious and pernicious character of Owen's writings and principles. The alleged modification of his views before death was not given the weight to which many thought it was entitled.*

His friends being thus prevented by local obstacles from erecting in the town of his birth and death a drinking fountain, clock tower, or other fitting memorial of the philanthropist, placed an obelisk in Kensal Green Cemetery, London,· and contented themselves with the memorial which had been placed in the Old Churchyard at Newtown, a simple table tombstone of blue flag surrounded by a low iron railing, with the following inscriptions on its four sides :—

'In Memory of
Robert Owen, the Philanthropist.
Born at Newtown, May 14, 1771.
Died at Newtown, Nov. 17, 1858.'

'Robert Owen,
Father of the Philanthropist.
Died March 14th, 1804.   Aged 65 years.'

---

* During his last stay in Newtown, immediately before his death, the Rev. John Edwards, then rector, frequently visited Owen, and also administered the Communion to him.

'Anne Owen,
Mother of the Philanthropist.
Died July 13th, 1803.    Aged 68 years.'
'Erected by Public Subscription, 1861.'

A few years ago a beautiful railing, composed of bronze and iron, standing upon a coping of local stone, from the design of Mr. Albert Toft, was placed around Owen's grave, bearing the following inscription :—

'To the memory of Robert Owen, founder of the Co-operative movement : This monument was erected by the Co-operative Union, acting on behalf of the Co-operators of the United Kingdom, 1902. "It is the one great and universal interest of the human race to be cordially united, and to aid each other to the full extent of their capacities." ROBERT OWEN.'

The principle feature is a bronze plaque bearing a relief symbolical of the life of Owen—he opens the Gate of Hope to the toiling artisan and operative. On either side are panels of wrought iron, one fitted with a slightly conventionalised arrangement of the Teazle, emblematic of work ; and the other with the Poppy, symbolising rest and sleep. Beneath the bronze plaque is a wrought-iron panel, the centre occupied by a wheel, spade, and pick, and other attributes of work, flanked on either side by vertical panels, the central feature of which is a cypher composed of two ' R. O.'s interlaced—the initial letters of Owen. At the back of the monumental rail is a portrait bust of Owen framed in wrought iron, the designs being composed of the palms and laurels of everlasting victory.

The ceremony of unveiling this memorial was performed by the late Mr. George Jacob Holyoake, the last surviving co-worker and friend of Robert Owen, who was also present in the ceremony on the day of Owen's burial.

By his wife, who predeceased him many years, Robert Owen had eight children.

Of a truth it may be said that Robert Owen was the greatest man, the ablest man, Newtown ever produced. He was the founder of infant schools, and advo-

cated for years the establishment of co-
operative stores, and, to all intents and
purposes, he was practically the originator
and founder of the principle in connection
with the commercial enterprises. To him
also we largely owe the factory acts and
municipal socialism. It was he who proposed the establishment of free libraries,
and suggested to the provincial authorities
that they should undertake the housing of
the poor.

Robert Owen, without a doubt, was one
of the strongest educative and inspiring
forces of the nineteenth century, and although
regarded by many as an impracticable
theorist, who tried to reorganise society
on an impossible basis, it cannot be denied
that his splendid example and many of his
teachings are needed to-day to emphasise
the importance of character in the education of the citizen. His career is one long
history of events in which self-denial
played an important part, and thanks to
the doctrines which he held and taught
knowledge is now greater, life longer,

health surer, disease limited, towns sweeter, hours of labour shorter, men stronger, women fairer, children happier, and industry held in more honour and better rewarded.

Owen's philanthropy was never questioned, even by his most determined opponents ; and his 'communism' or 'socialism,' as it was called, is no longer dreaded as the bugbear it once was deemed, seeing that the law favours 'limited liability,' which in its turn favours 'co-operation,' and co-operation is approved by the most respectable society, which goes in carriages to 'the stores.'

Partnership on the most extended scale—partnership on the enlarged plan of industrial societies and the like—was practically as much as Owen meant ; and his most visionary schemes have all been quietly accomplished, or rather have accomplished themselves in the course of time.

His views upon marriage were at one time much condemned. What Owen desired chiefly was to see marriage made a civil contract. It is so to-day, and marriages are now performed in a registrar's office as well as in a place of worship. He also advocated the law of divorce, a law which he wished to make similar to that which prevailed in America, rather than that which is now prevalent in this country.

It is true Owen was not a religious man in the sense generally associated with the word, yet no one was able to point to anything in his life, his character, or to find fault with him. He lived a good moral life, was wholly unselfish, and pre-eminently a gentleman. Under his refining influence the rough, untutored men who flocked to his standard became gentle too. When persecution came, they took it like their master, patiently and wisely. In his attitude towards religion, he assumed no hatred of old creeds. According to Lloyd Jones : 'He neither disputed the right nor questioned the sincerity of those who taught or professed them. His wife was a zealous believer in the religion in which

she was brought up, and he never disputed
or interfered with her desire to educate his
children in the creed she thought the best ;
and, therefore, when those who sought to
injure his character inquired as to his
habits and mode of life, they were informed
that the Bible was regularly read in the
New Lanark Schools, and that in his house
family prayer was a daily practice.'

Owen pictured as the most important
day of his life that on which bigotry, super-
stition, and all false religion received their
death blow. No doubt there is much in
his earlier writings and speeches which
Christian people may seriously repudiate ;
but, like Carlyle, he was a Free Thinker.
He can hardly be an infidel who declares
that he can ' trace the finger of God
directing his steps, preserving his life in
imminent danger, and compelling him on-
ward on many occasions,' or who speaks of
' a wise and good Creator.' These are the
words of the social reformer, of whom
Southey wrote : ' If I were his couutrymen
I would class him in the triad of the three

men who have in this generation given an impulse to the moral world, . . . . . his charity is a better plank than the faith of an intolerant and bitter-minded bigot, who, as Warburton says, counter-works his Creator, makes God after man's image, and chooses the worst model he can find—himself.'

Robert Owen was a man of whom any town should be proud to boast as being his birthplace. He was born to be great, and he achieved the natural tendency of his birth. Every man has his opportunity, and has left behind him the records as to its use or abuse. To Owen the happiness of the working people of this country was an all-absorbing thought, and his sole purpose was to alleviate the privations of the poorer classes, to make them feel that life was more than a drudge, and to teach them that true happiness was not to be found by trampling upon their weaker brethren, but was to be met with in earnest co-operation. He amassed fortunes and spent them for the benefit of those whom

he loved as quickly as they were obtained.
He might have become a millionaire, or
founded a county family, or he might have
obtained a peerage ; but Robert Owen
attained greater influence and celebrity than
either of these positions would have
brought him, and he felt justified in the
belief that he was at one time the most
popular man in England. In every effort
he made for the benefit of society his aims
were honest, his patriotism unimpeachable,
his generosity unbounded, his sacrifices
great and unhesitatingly subscribed. He
laboured for the people, he died working
for them, and his last thought was for their
welfare. Notwithstanding all this, it
appears that the folk of Newtown take
no particular pride in the fact that the
place is, at least, the home of one man
who forms part of the history of the nineteenth century, and it is little short of a
disgrace that the memory of a man whom
John Burns designates as ' the greatest
Britisher of the century and the most
powerful of formative influences of all

times,' who had the ear of the great leaders of the nation, and at request gave advice to foreign potentates, who was born and died at Newtown, should be allowed to pass away almost unnoticed.

'A prophet is not without honour save in his own country.'

Robert Owen published a large number of books and tracts, including—

A New View of Society, or Essays on the Formation of Human Character (1813).

Observations on the Cotton Trade of Great Britain (1815).

A Bill for Regulating the Hours of Work in Mills and Factories (1815).

Observations on the Effects of the Manufacturing System (1817).

A Letter to the Archbishop of Canterbury on the Union of Churches and Schools (1818).

A Letter to the Earl of Liverpool on the Employment of Children in Manufactories (1818).

Two Memorials on behalf of the Working Classes (1819).

An Address delivered to the Inhabitants of New Lanark on the 1st January, 1819, at the opening of the Institution for the Formation of Character.

The Book of the New Moral Work, containing the Rational System of Society (dedicated to King William IV).

The Life of Robert Owen, written by himself, with Selections from his Writings and Correspondence (1857).*

The Human Race Governed without Punishment (1858).

---

* There is a copy of this work in the Powysland Library at Welshpool, with the following characteristic inscription :—
'Presented to His Excellency the Saxon Ambassador to Great Britain by the Author, who has written these works with a view to open a new book of life to Man, and a greatly superior existence to the Human Race.
'Sevenoaks Park, Sevenoaks, 20 April, 1858.'

Milton Keynes UK
Ingram Content Group UK Ltd.
UKHW021956290923
429673UK00005B/160